RAF, DOMINION & ALLIED SQUADRONS AT WAR:
STUDY, HISTORY AND STATISTICS

COMPILED BY
PHIL H. LISTEMANN

Drawings by Claveworks Graphic

I0167778

PREFACE

The purpose of this study is to provide aviation historians and enthusiasts with a range of information relative to each of the Commonwealth squadrons that saw combat during World War II. Each record will comprise a short history, complete with illustrations and artwork, and accompanied by the following appendices:

Appendix I: Squadron Commanders and Flight Commanders
Appendix II: Major awards
Appendix III: Operational diary (number of sorties per month)
Appendix IV: Victory list
Appendix V: Aircraft losses on operations
Appendix VI: Aircraft losses in accidents
Appendix VII: Aircraft Serial numbers matching with individual letters (including mission totals for multi-engine aircraft)
Appendix VIII: Nominal roll (Captains only for bomber and seaplane units)
Appendix IX: Roll of Honour

Individual files will be constantly updated, when any fresh information comes to light. Additional information will be available for download, at no charge, on each squadron's site at:

www.RAF-IN-COMBAT.com

GLOSSARY OF TERMS

RANKS

AC: Aircraftman
G/C: Group Captain
W/C: Wing Commander
S/L: Squadron Leader
F/L: Flight Lieutenant
F/O: Flying Officer
P/O: Pilot Officer
W/O: Warrant Officer
F/Sgt: Flight Sergeant
Sgt: Sergeant
Cpl: Corporal
LAC: Leading Aircraftman

DFM: Distinguished Flying Medal
DSO: Distinguished Service Order
Eva.: Evaded
Inj.: Injured
ORB: Operational Record Book
OTU: Operational Training Unit
PAF: Polish Air Force
PoW: Prisoner of War
RAF: Royal Air Force
RAAF: Royal Australian Air Force
RCAF: Royal Canadian Air Force
RNZAF: Royal New Zealand Air Force
SAAF: South African Air Force
Sqn: Squadron
TOC: Taken on charge

OTHER

AAF: Auxiliary Air Force
CO: Commanding Officer
DFC: Distinguished Flying Cross

†: Killed

No. 309 (Polish) Squadron 1940-1947

ISBN: 978-2918590-58-3

Contributors & Acknowledgments:

Phill Jones, Grzegorz Korcz, Wilhelm Ratuszyski - www.polishsquadronsrembered.com, Przemyslaw Skulski, Roger Wallsgrove (Text consultant), Wojtek Zmyslony - www.polishairforce.pl

Copyright

© 2012 Philedition - Phil Listemann

Revised 2013

Cover: No.309 Squadron's Mustang IIIs flying in close formation shortly after the war.

MAIN EQUIPMENT

LYSANDER III	Nov.40 - Mar.43
MUSTANG I	Aug.42 - Feb.44
HURRICANE IV	Feb.44 - Apr.44
HURRICANE IIC	Apr.44 - Sep.44
MUSTANG I	Sep.44 - Nov.44
MUSTANG III	Oct.44 - Dec.46

SQUADRON CODE LETTERS:

AR
AUTUMN 40 - AUTUMN 42

WC
SPRING 44 - END

SQUADRON HISTORY

No.309 (Polish) Squadron was formed at Abbotsinch on **8 October 1940** as an army co-operation unit for work with the Polish Army in Scotland. This unit was somewhat unique as it was formed with non-British personnel, the only such one in Army Co-operation Command. The squadron, still under formation, moved to Renfrew one month later while technical and flying personnel began to arrive at the unit. The personnel was made up of Poles from various pre-war reconnaissance Polish units, backed by British officers and airmen. The squadron received Westland Lysander Mk. IIIs at the same time, the standard aircraft of this Command at that time. Training began at full scale during December, but it took time before reaching operational status, mainly because of the problem of communication with lack of English language knowledge and also flying tactics, obliging the pilots to follow another training course at an OTU. Training with the Polish Army commenced in February 1941 and by that time, 309 Sqn had become a full Polish unit. Training continued from Dunino, near St. Andrews (Scotland) and by end of 1941, the winds of change began to arrive when Army Co-operation Command decided to relinquish its obsolete Lysanders for Mustang Mk.Is, equipped to carry out tactical reconnaissance missions over occupied Europe. Mustangs began to arrive in July 1942 but at first only B Flight was converted, while a C Flight still flying Lysanders was added during 1942. However it was not before, on 5 December 1942, the squadron carried out its first operational sortie over France, completed by F/L Piotrowski and F/O Narewski. In 1943, other changes occurred, the first being the move to Kirknewton and at the same time, the conversion of A Flight onto Mustangs and the disbandment of C Flight. When in June 1943, Army Co-operation Command was disbanded, 309 Sqn was officially transferred to Fighter Command and not to the newly-formed No.2 TAF. It continued to carry out its reconnaissance sorties over the Continent from Snailwell from November 1943 onwards. However, staying within Fighter Command/ADGB meant as well that the role of the squadron would have to change and the last reconnaissance sorties were indeed recorded in January 1944. The following month, the squadron was converted to true fighter unit, receiving at first Hurricane Mk.IVs as a temporary measure, later replaced by Hurricane Mk.IIs but only to allow the pilots to become familiar with fighter flying tactics. At the same time, 309 moved back to Scotland for air defence duties. In October 1944, the Squadron was converted once again, receiving Mustang IIIs, already used by many other Polish Air Force fighter squadrons. Consequently, 309 became also unique in having flown the two major versions of the Mustang, the Allison and Merlin powered versions. In December 1944, the squadron moved to East Anglia and joined the other Polish Air Force Mustang squadrons and provided escorts to bombers until the end of the war, claiming four aircraft destroyed including three Me262s. The squadron remained within Fighter Command until **6 January 1947** and was then disbanded, being one of the last remaining Polish units at that time still operational.

SQUADRON BASES

Abbotsinch	07.10.40 - 06.11.40	Snailwell	24.11.43 - 23.04.44
Renfrew	06.11.40 - 08.05.41	Drem	23.04.44 - 14.11.44
Dunino	08.05.41 - 26.11.42	Peterhead	14.11.44 - 14.12.44
Findo Gask	26.11.42 - 10.03.43	Andrews Field	14.12.44 - 10.08.45
Kirknewton	10.03.43 - 03.06.43	Coltishall	10.08.45 - 09.10.45
Snailwell	03.06.43 - 06.11.43	Bradwell Bay	09.10.45 - 17.11.45
Wellingore	06.11.43 - 24.11.43	Coltishall	17.11.45 - 06.01.47

POLISH AIR FORCE

At the same time as a Polish government in exile was taking shape after September 199 while Poland was falling into German hands, the formation of Polish units in UK began to be discussed in association with the French and the British. However, England was ready to accept only a limited number of former Polish Air Force personnel, and at first only 2,300 personnel began to arrive in December 1939. Because of the geographical situation, it was decided to form two operational bomber squadrons (and two others in reserve) able to operate from British bases. The formation of these first Polish squadrons took time because of the slow arrival of the personnel and the need to retrain them and to learn the basics of the English language. The first Polish unit, No.300 Sqn, was officially formed on 1 July 1940. The collapse of France precipitated things and many Poles were evacuated from France including many airmen. Negotiations were undertaken by both parties, the British and the Poles. The latter wanted to have more autonomy for the Polish-manned squadrons and that became a major issue. Eventually this led to the 5 August 1940 agreement where basically an autonomous Polish Air Force (PAF) was created within the RAF. Soon, the PAF made a major contribution to the RAF's war efforts. During summer 1940, no fewer than nine squadrons were formed, with two bomber squadrons in July (Nos.300 and 301) and two fighter squadrons (Nos.302 & 303), followed by two other bomber squadrons (Nos.304 and 305) and one fighter squadron (No.306) in August, and one night fighter squadron in September (No.307). Later, a fifth fighter squadron (No.308) and eventually one Army co-operation squadron, No.309 were formed in October. The contribution of the Polish fighter units during the Battle of Britain is often seen as vital for the British, and the Poles distinguished themselves on many occasions. 303 Sqn became the top-scoring fighter squadron of the Battle of Britain. From that point, the British people had a moral debt to the Poles, something the British government had to deal with in 1945.

In 1941, the expansion of the PAF continued and new squadrons were formed, Nos.315, 316 and 317, all fighter units. A last PAF unit was eventually formed in 1943, No.318 Sqn, a tactical reconnaissance unit. Thus, the PAF became unique compared to the other foreign squadrons, in being a totally balanced air force with operational, fighters, bomber, night fighter, tactical and general reconnaissance units. The PAF fought with valour and courage and 1,900 Poles were killed to all causes between 1940 and 1945. The fighter pilots claimed close to 1,000 enemy aircraft destroyed over the same time.

By summer 1945, the political situation in Europe had changed, and more dramatically for the Poles. The British had to consider the fact that Poland had been 'liberated' by the Soviets, who had installed their own government in Warsaw, and thus on 6 July 1945, the British government stopped recognising the legal Polish government in London. Consequently the Polish Armed Forces in Britain, including the PAF, were absorbed into the British forces until arrangements for their demobilisation could be completed. However, the Polish government in exile continued to be recognised by the Poles in exile and this became a major political but also ethical issue for the British, split between their will to see the Polish units disbanded and the fact that only a few Poles had indicated an intention to return home, under Soviet control, embarrassing at the least for the British government who hoped to sort it out without trouble. With the help the Poles provided to the British people in 1940 still in mind, the British were obliged not to leave the Poles without a dignified way out. A Polish Resettlement Corps (PRC) for the Polish forces was formed in the following months to help the Poles who didn't want to return to Poland to find a solution. The process of disbandment of Polish squadrons was long, involving various stages during 1946, with things accelerating in autumn 1946. By 6 January 1947, the PAF had ceased to exist. Despite this, many Poles still had to be resettled, as of 14,350 Poles of the PAF recorded in May 1945, only 3,000 had chosen to return in Poland. For many of them a tragic fate was waiting, as they were not welcomed and were often seen as spies for the Western countries. The bulk remained in the UK including 500 who eventually joined the RAF. Many later choose to emigrate to other Commonwealth countries but also to the USA, Argentina.

APPENDIX I
SQUADRON AND FLIGHT COMMANDERS

Rank and Name	SN	Origin	Dates
W/C Neville M.F. **MASON**	RAF No.16114	RAF	07.10.40 - 24.11.40
W/C Zygmunt **PISTL**	PAF P-0475	PAF	24.11.40 - 14.02.43
S/L Witold **PIOTROWSKI**	RAF No.76687	(POL)/RAF	14.02.43 - 14.10.43
S/L Maciej **PIOTROWSKI**	PAF P-0003	PAF	14.10.43 - 02.04.44
S/L Jerzy **GOLKO**	RAF No.76655	(POL)/RAF	02.04.44 - 09.09.44
S/L Antoni **GLOWACKI**	PAF P-1527	PAF	09.09.44 - 16.07.45
S/L Henryk **PIETRZAK**	PAF P-1915	PAF	16.07.45 - 06.01.47

A FLIGHT

	SN	Origin	Dates
F/L Fidelis J. **ŁUKASIK** [1]	PAF P-1054	PAF	Nov.40 - Oct.41
F/L Julian **ŁAGOWSKI**	PAF P-0899	PAF	Oct.41 - 01.03.43
F/L Jerzy **GOLKO**	RAF No.76655	(POL)/RAF	01.03.43 - 02.04.44
F/L Jan **WIŚNIEWSKI**	PAF P-0899	PAF	02.04.44 - Jun.44
F/L Mieczysław **LEWANDOWSKI**	PAF P-0010	PAF	Jun.44 - Nov.44
F/L Jerzy **MENCEL**	PAF P-0217	PAF	Nov.44 - 25.05.45
F/L Wlodzimierz **KLAWE**	PAF P-0387	PAF	25.05.45 - 26.03.46
F/L Tadeusz **BUDZICH**	PAF P-2724	PAF	26.03.46 - 06.01.47

[1] backed by F/L L.B. Egon-Mayer

B FLIGHT

	SN	Origin	Dates
F/L Alexander **ŁUKIŃSKI** [1]	PAF P-1421	PAF	Nov.40 - 11.03.44
F/L Maciej **PIOTROWSKI**	PAF P-0003	PAF	June 42 - 01.03.43
F/L Jan **NAREWSKI**	PAF P-0799	PAF	01.03.43 - 21.03.43
F/L Janusz **LEWKOWICZ**	PAF P-0677	PAF	21.03.43 - 13.08.44
F/L Jan **SZYSZKO**	PAF P-0112	PAF	Jun.44 - 20.11.45
F/L Mieczyslaw **GORZULA**	RAF No.76695	(POL)/RAF	20.11.44 - 07.08.45
F/L Karol **BIRTUS**	PAF P-1711	PAF	07.08.45 - 06.01.47

[1] backed by F/L W. Bundock

C FLIGHT

	SN	Origin	Dates
F/L Tadeusz **KERN**	PAF P-0359	PAF	01.02.42 - *n/k*
F/L Jan **HRYNIEWICZ**	PAF P-0056	PAF	*n/k* - 23.02.43

APPENDIX II
MAJOR AWARDS

DSO: -

DFC: 1
Jerzy Stanisław **MENCEL** (PAF P-0217 - PAF)

DFM: -

Date	Pilot	SN	Origin	Type	Serial	Code	Nb	Cat.

APPENDIX III
Operational Diary
Number of Sorties per Month

Date	Month	Total	Date	Month	Total
Dec.42	16	16			
Jan.43	2	18	May.44	30	410
Feb.43	14	32	Jun.44	50	460
Mar.43	6	38	Jul.44	50	510
.../...			Aug.44	36	546
Jun.43	4	42	Sep.44	24	570
Jul.43	50	92	Oct.44	18	588
Aug.43	68	160	Nov.44	4	592
Sep.43	18	178	Dec.44	64	656
Oct.43	51	229	Jan.45	103	759
Nov.43	48	277	Feb.45	140	899
Dec.43	67	344	Mar.45	217	1,116
Jan.44	32	376	Apr.45	163	1,279
.../...					
Apr.44	4	380	**Grand Total**		**1,279**

Extracted from AIR27/1679

APPENDIX IV
Victory list
confirmed (C) and probable (P) claims

MUSTANG III

Date	Pilot	S/N	Origin	Mark	Serial	Code		Fate
21.02.45	W/O Antoni **Murkowski**	PAF 784755	PAF	Fw190D	**FX853**	WC-W	1.0	C
09.04.45	W/O Antoni **Murkowski**	PAF 784755	PAF	Me262	**FB385**	WC-W	1.0	C
	F/L Mieczysław **Gorzula**	RAF No.76695	(POL)/RAF	Me262	**FZ111**	WC-V	1.0	C
	F/L Jerzy **Mencel**	PAF P-0217	PAF	Me262	**KH516**	WC-F	1.0	C

Total: 4.0

Aircraft damaged: 2.0

APPENDIX V
Aircraft Lost on Operations

Date	Pilot	S/N	Origin	Serial	Code	Mark	Fate

MUSTANG

Date	Pilot	S/N	Origin	Serial	Code	Mark	Fate
03.01.44	F/O Roman **Jarema**	PAF P-1559	PAF	**AP217**	F	I	-

Eight Mustangs took off at 11.05 led by S/L Piotrowski for a shipping recce along the Dutch coast between Ijmuiden and Den Helder. The mission was uneventful, however Jarema crashed on landing owing to engine failure. The pilot was injured in the left eye and was admitted to hospital. Jarema had joined the squadron during summer 1942. He left the squadron the following November and had 12 months unpaid leave in order to continue his medical studies. He stayed in the UK after the war.

Note on the aircraft: Arrived in UK on 02.07.42. Issued to No.309 Sqn 16.11.42.

19.03.45   F/L Stanisław **SAWICKI**   PAF P-1576   PAF   **FX860**   WC-P   III   †

F/L Sawicki took off with the squadron as No.4 in Blue Section to escort 18 Lancasters targeting Vlotho viaduct (RAMROD 1504). The squadron was led by W/C K. Rutkowski. The take-off took place at 08.30. Shortly after setting course, grey smoke was seen coming from his engine exhaust and the Mustang began to lose speed. He apparently decided to return and turned to the left and made a forced landing in a soft field near Broomfield, Essex with his auxiliary tank still on. The fuel ignited on contact and set fire to the aircraft which was destroyed. Sawicki was badly burned and was rescued by patients of the nearby hospital, but eventually died of his wounds around 18.00 the same day. (see also 19.10.44 - aircraft lost in accident)

Note on the aircraft: Built as P-51B-1-NA 43-12312, stored at No.19 MU from 19.11.43 until being issued to No.309 Sqn on 23.10.44.

Total: 2

APPENDIX VI
AIRCRAFT LOST IN ACCIDENTS

Date	Pilot	S/N	Origin	Serial	Code	Mark	Fate

LYSANDER

04.02.41   P/O Roman **SUWALSKI**   RAF No.76757   (POL)/RAF   **R9134**   III   -

During a training flight, P/O Roman Suwalski crashed on landing at Dumfries, the pilot escaping major injuries. The crash is some times reported to have occurred on the 6th, but it was chosen the date reported in the ORB. Roman Suwalski was a former Polish Air Force pilot who fought against the Germans in September 1939 and escaped later to the United Kingdom. He joined the squa -dron in November 1940 and soon after this accident, he was posted to No.275 Sqn flying Lysanders. At the end of 1941, he was sent to No.57 OTU to convert as a fighter pilot, but was killed in a flying accident on 26.01.42 whilst flying Spitfire Mk.I X4164.

Note on the aircraft: TOC No.39 MU 05.08.40. Issued No.309 Sqn 02.11.40.

04.05.41   P/O Teofil **SZYMANKIEWICZ**   PAF P-0744   PAF   **T1739**   III   -
              Unidentified observer   -

Swung on landing at Arbroath and pilot failed to correct. This occurred during an air exercise code named 'Forfar' which took place on the east coast of Scotland between the 2-4 May. The date of the accident is reported as the 2th May in the ORB, and not the 4th as the accident card stated. Both crewmen were uninjured. Teofil Szymankiewicz fought the Germans in September 1939 then flew to Romania then reached France. He enlisted in the French Air Force and did not fly in operations. He then escaped to Great Britain, joining the squadron in November 1940. In October 1941 he left the squadron and converted into a fighter pilot. He was posted to No.306 (Polish) Sqn in November 1941 and No.316 (Polish) Sqn soon after and finally No.317 (Polish) Sqn in April 1942. He completed his tour in December 1942. In June 1944, he started another tour with No.316 (Polish) Sqn and served until he was killed on 02.01.45 flying Mustang III KH494 while doing an approach to Heesch (Holland) in bad weather.

Note on the aircraft: TOC No.37 MU 26.11.40, issued No.309 Sqn 07.04.41.

18.06.41   Sgt Zymunt **KOWALCZYK**   PAF 793719   PAF   **V9608**   IIIA   -
              F/L Aleksander **ŁUKIŃSKI**   PAF P-1421   PAF   -

Crashed at the aerodrome at Dunino and totally destroyed by fire. During a dive bombing practice flight over the aerodrome, the Very pistol exploded in the cockpit and obliged the pilot to make an emergency landing. Kowalczyk a pre-war PAF pilot and was an experienced pilot with 500 hours logged in Poland plus 72 in the UK including 58 on type. Both crew suffered slight injuries. Zygmunt Kowalczyk later served with No.305 Sqn and survived the war. Lukinski was also a pre-war PAF member and like Kowalczyk later served with No.305 Sqn. But unlike Kowalczyk, he did not survived the war, being killed as navigator in Mosquito FB.VI LR300 during the night of 10/11.07.44 while carrying out an intruder sortie over France.

Note on the aircraft: TOC No.37 MU 28.04.41, issued No.309 Sqn 24.05.41.

25.02.42   F/O Piotr **DUNIN**   PAF P-1353   PAF   **V9472**   IIIA   ✝

           F/O Jerzy **HOMAN**   PAF P-0757   PAF   ✝

Since the previous day, the Squadron had been participating in an exercise with the 1st Guards Brigade. That day, F/O Dunin was practising dive bombing on gun position when for unknown reasons the aircraft failed to recover from a dive, killing the crew instantly. Dunin participated to the Battle of Poland in September as a liaison pilot. He fled to France when he was trained on Martin 167s but never flew on operations. He found his way to the UK and re-trained and posted to No.309 Sqn in November 1940. Jerzy Homan was still under training when the Germans invaded Poland. It is not sure if he reached France before reaching England, but he was serving with the squadron since November 1940, like Dunin.

Note on the aircraft: TOC No.37 MU 24.02.41, issued No.309 Sqn 09.05.41.

MUSTANG

08.05.43   F/L Jan **SZYSZKO**   PAF P-0112   PAF   **AM213**   I   -

Returning from an air-to-air firing exercise and just prior to touch down at Peterhead at 12.15, the aircraft swung to port and the pilot failed to correct . The port wing touched the ground on landing and dug in, the pilot escaping injuries. The pilot's little experience on the type (less than 40 hours) was probably the main cause of the accident. Szyszko was serving with the squadron since September 1942 and left two years later in September 1944. He later returned to the squadron after VE-Day (see 08.08.45 - aircraft lost in accident).

Note on the aircraft: Arrived in UK 12.07.42. Issued No.309 Sqn 19.08.42.

27.12.43   F/O Eugeniusz **RAJEWSKI**   PAF P-1572   PAF   **AP240**   G   I   ✝

Crashed and caught fire after engaging in a mock dog fight with an American P-38 Lightning. This dogfight was not authorised and occurred under 4,000 feet. It seems that the aircraft stalled after a tight turn and due to the low altitude, Rajewski was unable to recover in time. Eugeniusz Rajewski had joined the squadron in May 1942. He was born in the United States from Polish immigrants. He had sailed to the UK in 1940 and enlisted in the RAF after the fall of Poland.

Note on the aircraft: Arrived in UK 23.07.42. Issued No.309 Sqn 18.11.42.

HURRICANE

28.09.44   F/O Julian **STRUSIŃSKI**   PAF P-0979   PAF   **LF633**   WC-T   IIC   ✝

F/O Strusinski took off at 10.40 to practice with other aircraft of the squadron a formation flying and cine camera gun exercise. At 11.15, Strusinski was doing a cine camera gun exercise when the pilot of the other aircraft pressed the gun button in error for camera button and shot Strusinksi's aircraft down in flames into the sea two miles E of Peterhead. Strusinski participated to the Polish campaign as a technical officer before fleeing to France. Once more he fled, this time to the UK where he served as technical officer with No.316 Sqn before joining a pilot's course in January 1942. He later served with various second line units like No.1601 Flt and was posted to No.309 Sqn in May 1944.

Note on the aircraft: TOC No.22 MU 02.03.44. Issued to No.309 Sqn 21.05.44 after having served with Nos.63 & 289 Sqns.

MUSTANG

18.10.44   F/L Władysław **GORZEŃSKI**   PAF P-2397   PAF   **AP213**   WC-O   I   -

F/L Gorzenski took off from Peterhead when at about 100 feet, his engine cut with smoke coming from the exhaust pipes. After operating the throttle, the engine picked up again but once more cut out. In order to avoid landing in a small ravine, he decided to land without flaps. Still trying to save the aircraft, by operating throttle and rpm, he eventually made a belly landing at Barrydown Farm, Aberdeenshire. The aircraft caught fire and the fuselage forwards of the cockpit was completely burnt out, Gorzenski escaping injuries. He had joined the squadron in July 1944 and had served previously with No.315 Sqn. He left the squadron soon after this accident. After the war he emigrated to Canada in 1948.

Note on the aircraft: Arrived in UK 02.07.42. Served with Nos.16, 168, 4 and 414 (RCAF) Sqns before to be issued to No.309 Sqn 30.09.44.

19.10.44   F/L Stanisław **SAWICKI**   PAF P-1576   PAF   **AP177**   I   -

After an aircraft test flight, the pilot forgot to select the undercarriage down and the controller didn't warn the pilot that he was to preparing to land without the undercarriage down. The aircraft eventually belly landed at Drem at 16.30. Born in Odessa in Russia, Sawicki was a long-time member of No.309 Sqn, joining in November 1940. He remained with the squadron until February 1944 (except for two weeks in August 1942 to fly a Mustang Mk.I with 26 Sqn) when he became liaison PAF officer with the 1st Polish Armoured Division and returned to the squadron in November 1944. Later killed while serving the squadron. (see also 19.03.45 - operational losses)

Note on the aircraft: Arrived in UK 16.07.42.Served with Nos.613 & 63 Sqns before to be issued to No.309 Sqn 27.09.44.

27.10.44   F/L Wincenty **MINISZEWSKI**   PAF P-1568   PAF   **AP170**   WC-M   I   -

During an aircraft test, the engine of the aircraft failed due to the air filters collapsing, and as the pilot was unable to keep altitude he chose to make an emergency landing near Mains Farm, Ballincrieff, East Lothian, at 10.00. Miniszewski was serving with the squadron since August 1942. He left soon after this incident and did not fly on Mustang IIIs as a fighter pilot.

Note on the aircraft: Arrived in UK 10.08.42.Served with Nos.239 & 430 (RCAF) Sqns before to be issued to No.309 Sqn 30.09.44.

18.02.45   F/L Kazimierz **ZIELONKA**   PAF P-1742   PAF   **SR418**   WC-D   III   -

F/L Kazimierz Zielonka had taken off with other Mustangs to carry out training formation and battle attacks. He was making a dummy attack on another section of Mustangs when two USAAF Thunderbolts appeared and began to attack the Mustangs. The Thunderbolt of Lt Byron J. Fisher, of the 61st FS/56th FG (P-47M-1-RE 44-21161), collided with Zielonka's aircraft and exploded killing the American pilot. Zielonka baled out and landed safely but with injuries which obliged him to be taken to hospital at the Black Notkey facilities. Zielonka had just joined the squadron. He later emmigrated to the USA.

Note on the aircraft: Built as P-51B-1-NA 43-12188, transferred from 8th AF stock 29.03.44, modified to RAF standard and stored until being issued to No.309 Sqn 27.10.44.

16.05.45   F/L Franciszek **KUBICA**   PAF P-2135   PAF   **FB383**   WC-X   III   †

During a practice interception exercise with No.306 Sqn over the North Sea, the two aircraft collided at 18,000 feet at 10.45. The two pilots were able to evacuate their aircraft and two parachutes were seen coming down into the sea and an ASR mission was launched immediately. During the whole of the afternoon and the next morning, Kubica was searched for intensively but he was never located. Kubica was with the squadron since July 1944.

Note on the aircraft: Built as P-51C-5-NT, sailed on S.S. *British Flory*, reaching UK 04.05.44. Served with No.316 (Polish) Sqn before being issued to No.309 Sqn 05.04.45.

            F/L Mieczysław **BEFINGER**   PAF P-1896   PAF   **KH540**   WC-D   III   †

See above. The ASR mission found Befinger's body at14.20. His dinghy was not with him, but was half inflated 100 yards away. 'Czechy' Befinger served with the squadron for a long time, having joined in August 1942.

Note on the aircraft: Built as P-51C-10-NT 44-10965, sailed on S.S. *Empire Juventor*, reaching UK 24.08.44. Stored before to be issued to No.309 Sqn 02.03.45.

02.08.45   W/O Aleksander **PIETRZAK**   PAF 783147   PAF   **FX876**   WC-D   III   †

At 10.15, the squadron took off to carry out various exercises (close formation dive bombing and battle formation), when during take-off W/O Pietrzak reported to the CO that his aircraft was not responding to the rudder and the CO ordered him to land. He replied that he would do so and rejoin the formation in another aircraft. However, after 3 or 4 minutes, Pietrzak rejoined the formation and reported that his aircraft was alright to continue the flight. After close formation, the squadron proceeded to carry out dive bombing practice over the airfield and Pierrzak's aircraft, when travelling at 300-350 mph, was observed to increase the diving angle and at the same time turning to the left. Gradually the aircraft turned onto its back reaching a speed of about 530 mph. At about 30-50 feet above the airfield the aircraft went to a level position but still inverted and then pulled up violently. Immediately after the pull-up, the pilot was seen to fall from the aircraft and was killed instantly. The Mustang climbed to 3,000 feet and then went into the ground vertically and crashed in a field on Gould's Farm, Rayne, near Braintree. It is believed that the main cause of the accident was the malfunction of the rudder. Aleksander Pietrzak, who had joined the squadron in February 1945, was a very experienced pilot who escaped to the UK after the fall of Poland and was trained as a pilot and joined No.302 (Polish) Sqn in 1943 with which he claimed a Fw190 as destroyed. He ended his tour early in 1944, and started another tour with No.316 (Polish) Sqn on Mustangs in June 1944 and added three Bf109s to his tally – one being shared – and four V-1s.

Note on the aircraft: Built as P-51B-1-NA 42-12146, sailed on S.S. *F.J. Wolfe* reaching UK on 23.09.43. Served with Nos.316 & 129 Sqns and FIU before being issued to No.309 Sqn on 24.05.45.

08.08.45   F/O Zygmunt **JAESCHKE**   PAF P-2700   PAF   **FZ184**   III   -

F/O Jaeschke was detailed that day to carry out an air test and as the aircraft took-off the engine backfired and cut. There was no time for the pilot to do anything but force land at 11.15 straight ahead and this he did with the undercarriage down, but the port oleo struck a tree stump and was ripped off. Zygmunt Jaeschke fled from Poland to Hungary at the age of 17 in September 1939. He reached France in 1940 and joined the Polish Army with which he fought during the Battle of France. He was evacuated to the UK with his regiment. He volunteered to serve with the PAF in 1943 and after having served in second line units joined No.309 Sqn in September 1944. After the war he returned in Poland.
Note on the aircraft: Built as P-51B-5-NA 43-6605, sailed on S.S. *Lerncourt*, reaching UK on 22.11.43. Served with Nos.122, 19 & 129 Sqns before to be issued to No.309 Sqn 10.05.45.

15.10.45   Sgt Stanisław **ŚWIĘCICKI**   PAF 706191   PAF   **KH516**   WC-F   III   †

Sgt Swiecicki took off at 13.25 to carry out dive bombing practice. 15 minutes later, whilst diving on to the target his aircraft was seen to break up in the air and crashed on Dengie Flats range (Essex) killing its pilot. It is believed that structural failure was the cause of the crash. A brutal action may have overstressed the aircraft or the elevator trim. A fresh graduate, Swiecicki had joined the squadron on VE-Day.
Note on the aircraft: Built as P-51C-10-NT 44-10918, sailed on S.S. *E.J. Nicholson*, reaching UK on 17.08.44. Served with No.316 (Polish) Sqn before being issued to No.309 Sqn on 01.03.45.

30.11.45   Sgt Józef **PODOLSKI**   PAF 705716   PAF   **FB232**   III   -

The pilot was returning from B.58 together with F/O Stankiewicz who was leading. Unfortunately the R/T of Stankiewicz failed during the flight and Podolski had to take the lead. Owing to bad weather at Coltishall the two Mustangs were vectored to West Raynham. Podoloski lost Stankiewicz in the clouds over West Raynham. The visibility was very poor, so much that the pilot could not see the lights of the airfield properly. Having no idea which direction he should take to land, he asked for a vector for landing and received vector 22. He made 11 approaches to land without receiving indications that he was approaching for the wrong direction; he eventually landed downwind, overshot and crashed. The pilot was not hurt but was later admitted to hospital suffering from shock. A freshly graduated fighter pilot, Podolski had joined the squadron a couple of weeks earlier.
Note on the aircraft: Built as P-51C-1-NT 42-103126, sailed on S.S. *Doncella* and reached UK on 27.01.44. Served with Nos.316 (Polish), 122, 65, 129 Sqns before to be issued to No.309 Sqn 24.05.45.

16.01.46   W/O Tadeusz **WIŚNIEWSKI**   PAF 782739   PAF   **KH484**   WC-H   III   -

W/O Wiśniewski took off in the evening for a night navigation exercise when after 1 hour and minutes of flight, the engine failed and white smoke was seen to come from the engine compartment. The pilot attempted to restart the engine and when this failed, changed fuel tanks and tried again without success. At 800 feet, he jettisoned the external stores and attempted to make a forced landing at 17.55, but faced with a built up area, he landed the Mustang on wooded ground and it was destroyed. Wiśniewski had previously served with No.308 (Polish) Sqn before joining the squadron at the end of May 1945 .
Note on the aircraft: Built as P-51C-10-NT 44-10841, reached UK 10.08.44. Never issued to any unit before being issued to No.309 Sqn on 08.03.45.

12.02.46   F/O Leonard **KRUŚ**   PAF P-2659   PAF   **FB210**   WC-P   III   †

At 10.00 F/O Krus took off for a squadron formation exercise. At 11.15, the aircraft broke away from the formation, shortly before entering cloud. The aircraft subsequently crashed out of control killing the pilot. It is believed that Krus had lost control when flying on instruments. Krus had joined the squadron after VE-Day.
Note on the aircraft: Built as P-51C-5-NT 42-103104, sailed on S.S. *British Gratitude*, reached UK 04.05.44. Stored until issued to No.309 Sqn on 23.10.44.

25.02.46   F/L Jan **MOZOŁOWSKI**   PAF P-1690   PAF   **KH473**   III   -

F/L Mozolowski took at 09.50 to carry out camera gun exercises and dogfights. About one hour later, he started a dogfight with S/L Pietrzak. During the course of the dogfight he completed a few turns and then in taking avoiding action he started a dive and almost at the same time the engine cut out, smoke started to appear and the windscreen became covered by oil. He opened the hood and being in the vicinity of the airfield came into land with the undercarriage down. However while at 60 feet, the aircraft stalled and struck the ground heavily and both u/c legs came off. The pilot escaped injuries. Declared Cat. B the aircraft was not repaired. Mozolowski had previously served with No.302 (Polish) Sqn in 1942-1943 and had joined the squadron in May 1944 for another tour.
Note on the aircraft: Built as P-51C-10-NT 44-10830, sailed on S.S. *White lines*, reached UK 18.08.44. Served with Nos.118 & 126 before being issued to No.309 Sqn on 09.08.45.

Tiger Moth

11.02.42	Capt James G.C. **Worledge**	98211	Army	**T6761**	I	†
	F/O Jerzy **Sadowski**	PAF P-0737	PAF			†

Having taken off on a liaison flight, the Tiger Moth fell into the sea in the waters of the Firth of Clyde at the heights of Toward Point. The pilot, Capt James Worledge of the Intelligence Corps and the British liaison officer and Jerzy Sadowski were both killed; Sadowski, the observer pilot, was in the squadron since November 1940.

Note on the aircraft: TOC No.46 MU 10.10.41. Issued No.309 Sqn 03.11.41.

Total: 22
including 21 combat aircraft

APPENDIX VII
Aircraft serial numbers matching with individual letters

AR/WC-A
AM221 (*Mustang I*)
LF620 (*Hurricane II*)
KH574, SR439 (*Mustang III*)
AR/WC-B
V9441 (*Lysander III*)
AM211, AP219* (*Mustang I*)
LF631, LF695 (*Hurricane II*)
FB118, FB143 (*Mustang III*)
AR/WC-C
AG600*, AM214 (*Mustang I*)
FB114, FX786, FX969 (*Mustang III*)
AR/WC-D
AG435 (*Mustang I*)
LF644 (*Hurricane II*)
KH540, SR418 (*Mustang III*)
AR/WC-E
AG648 (*Mustang I*)
LF658 (*Hurricane II*)
AR/WC-F
AP217 (*Mustang I*)
LF363, LF652 (*Hurricane II*)
FX885, KH516 (*Mustang III*)
AR/WC-G
AP240 (*Mustang I*)
LF331 (*Hurricane II*)
FX969 (*Mustang III*)
AR/WC-H
AM119 (*Mustang I*)
LF634 (*Hurricane II*)
KH484, SR408 (*Mustang III*)
AR/WC-I

AR/WC-J
AG499*, AM195 (*Mustang I*)
LF650 (*Hurricane II*)
FX930, FZ120 (*Mustang III*)
AR/WC-K
AG561, AP182* (*Mustang I*)
LF705 (*Hurricane II*)
FX908 (*Mustang III*)
AR/WC-L
AG423, AG621* (*Mustang I*)
LF647, LF707 (*Hurricane II*)
FX936 (*Mustang III*)
AR/WC-M
V9484 (*Lysander III*)
AG628, AP170* (*Mustang I*)
LF657 (*Hurricane II*)
SR420 (*Mustang III*)
AR/WC-N
V9576 (*Lysander III*)
AG635*, AL964 (*Mustang I*)
AR/WC-O
V9544 (*Lysander III*)
AG389, AP213* (*Mustang I*)
LF685 (*Hurricane II*)
FB210 (*Mustang III*)
AR/WC-P
AM165 (*Mustang I*)
LF637 (*Hurricane II*)
FB210, FX860 (*Mustang III*)
AR/WC-Q
AG589 (*Mustang I*)
AR/WC-R
AP226 (*Mustang I*)

LF699 (*Hurricane II*)
FB363, FX962 (*Mustang III*)
AR/WC-S
AM149*, AP226 (*Mustang I*)
LF630 (*Hurricane II*)
FB104, FX925 (*Mustang III*)
AR/WC-T
V9550 (*Lysander III*)
AP249 (*Mustang I*)
LF633 (*Hurricane II*)
FZ126, FZ171 (*Mustang III*)
AR/WC-U
PG429 (*Hurricane II*)
AR/WC-V
V9437 (*Lysander III*)
FZ111 (*Mustang III*)
AR/WC-W
AL987 (*Mustang I*)
PG428 (*Hurricane II*)
FB385, FX853 (*Mustang III*)
AR/WC-X
AG616 (*Mustang I*)
FB383, FZ124, SR419 (*Mustang III*)
AR/WC-Y
LF342 (*Hurricane II*)
FZ175 (*Mustang III*)
AR/WC-Z
LF335 (*Hurricane II*)
FB171 (*Mustang III*)

*Mustang I coded 'WC', otherwise no squadron codes

PAF

A.J. **Adamczak**, PAF P-0960
E. **Antolak**, PAF P-0232
A. **Barański**, PAF P-0680
B. **Baster**, PAF P-0538
M. **Bączalski**, PAF 707115
A.S. **Bączek**, PAF P-1891
M. **Befinger**, PAF P-1896
J. **Bendix**, PAF P-1539
W. **Bereżecki**, PAF P-0209
C.A. **Bernat**, PAF P-0806
A. **Beyer**, PAF P-0209
S. **Białkowski**, PAF 705557
S.K. **Birtus**, PAF P-1711
E. **Blok**, PAF P-2992
K. **Bokowiec**, PAF P-0492
T. **Budzich**, PAF P-2724
T. **Ciuła**, PAF 794977
W. **Chrzanowski**, PAF P-0134
B. **Chudziński**, PAF P-2399
T. **Cybulski**, PAF P-1795
I. **Czajka**, PAF P-2307
S. **Czerni**, PAF P-0952
A. **Czernecki**, PAF P-1714
B. **Czerwiński**, PAF 792271
S. **Dadej**, PAF P-1546
S.J. **Daniel**, PAF P-0735
P.J. **Dunin**, PAF P-1353
E.W. **Eisenbach**, PAF 704594
J.C. **Gadkowski**, PAF 706596
T. **Galler**, PAF P-0485
P. **Gallus**, PAF 794124
C.Z. **Gierycz**, PAF P-1753
A. **Głowacki**, PAF P-1527
R. **Godlewski**, PAF 704882
W. **Gorczyński**, PAF 704536
W. **Gorzeński**, PAF P-2397
J.E. **Grodziński**, PAF P-2387
E.K. **Hanka**, PAF 704206
J. **Homan**, PAF P-0757
J. **Hryniewicz**, PAF P-0056
Z.W. **Jaeschke**, PAF P-2700
R.S. **Jarema**, PAF P-1559
A. **Judek**, PAF P-2657
Z. **Jurek**, PAF 707323
L. **Kaczmarek**, PAF 792320
H. **Kamiński**, PAF P-2090
K. **Karaszewski**, PAF P-1858
Z. **Kawnik**, PAF P-2440

A. **Kempny**, PAF 705611
T. **Kern**, PAF P-0359
M.W. **Klawe**, PAF P-0387
R.N. **Kogut**, PAF 706168
W. **Korzeniewicz**, PAF P-1561
A. **Krakowski**, PAF P-0698
L. **Kruś**, PAF P-2659
F. **Kubica**, PAF P-2135
T.T. **Kulecki**, PAF 703977
B. **Kuźniar**, PAF P-0759
Z.J. **Kowalczyk**, PAF 793719
J. **Lemieszonek**, PAF P-1334
M.J. **Lewandowski**, PAF P-0010
J.J. **Lewkowicz**, PAF P-0677
E. **Loska**, PAF 782825
R. **Łopacki**, PAF 705600
F.J. **Łukasik**, PAF P-1054
A. **Łukiński**, PAF P-1421
W. **Madejski**, PAF P-1241
J. **Majer**, PAF P-0127
H.W. **Majewski**, PAF P-2136
J.A. **Maleńczuk**, PAF 793842
M. **Matus**, PAF 793620
J.S. **Mencel**, PAF P-0217
H. **Mikusek**, PAF 784021
K. **Miller**, PAF P-0710
W.J. **Miniszewski**, PAF P-1568
J.Z. **Mozołowski**, PAF P-1690
A.S. **Murkowski**, PAF 784755
J. **Narewski**, PAF P-0799
F. **Nienartowicz**, PAF 793743
W. **Olszewski**, PAF 706406
J. **Paciorkowski**, PAF P-0502
A. **Paradowski**, PAF 784203
A. **Piaskowski**, PAF P-2071
A. **Pietrzak**, PAF 783147
A. **Pietrzak**, PAF P-1915
E. **Pietrzyk**, PAF P-0850
M. **Piotrowski**, PAF P-0003
Z. **Pistl**, PAF P-0475
I. **Pisuliński**, PAF P-0866
J. **Podolski**, PAF 705716
A. **Polek**, PAF P-0790
Z. **Poraziński**, PAF P-0542
W. **Potocki**, PAF P-1856
A. **Powierza**, PAF P-1355
J. **Radziszewski**, PAF P-1736
E.L. **Rajewski**, PAF P-1572, *USA*
Z. **Rembowski**, PAF P-0522
J.P. **Sadowski**, PAF P-0737

J. **Salski**, PAF P-0737, *Ukrainia*
S. **Sawicki**, PAF P-1576
Z. **Sawicki**, PAF P-0884
E. **Sokołowski**, PAF P-0745
A. **Solecki**, PAF P-0574
Z. **Stankiewicz**, PAF P-2678
K.R. **Stefanus**, PAF P-0664
Z. **Stranz**, PAF P-0902
J. **Strusiński**, PAF P-0979
A.L. **Sulikowski**, PAF 703961
L.T. **Szczepański**, PAF 792472
T. **Szymankiewicz**, PAF P-0744
W. **Szypulewski**, PAF 782470
J.T. **Szyszko**, PAF P-0112
C. **Śnieć**, PAF P-1623
S. **Święcicki**, PAF 706191
E. **Tacik**, PAF P-1776
T.S. **Turek**, PAF P-2217
M. **Urban**, PAF P-1694
M.J. **Urbański**, PAF P-0627
T. **Wiśniewski**, PAF 782839
Z. **Wdowczyński**, PAF 794116
R.F. **Wojdała**, PAF 793797
H. **Wojtkiewicz**, PAF 781419
J.S. **Wolf**, PAF P-1244
S. **Zagroba**, PAF 704846
S. **Zajchowski**, PAF P-2294
S. **Zajdel**, PAF P-1698
J. **Zaleński**, PAF 780769
S.J. **Zaufal**, PAF P-2752
K. **Zielonka**, PAF P-1742
T.M. **Żeligowski**, PAF P-1497

RAF

E.W. **Bundock**, RAF No.39779
J.B. **Egan-Wyer**, RAF No.3428
J. **Gołko**, RAF No.76655, *Poland*
S. **Maciejewski**, RAF No.76679, *Poland*
N.M.F. **Mason**, RAF No.16114
L. **Mathias**, RAF No.33270
R. **Suwalski**, RAF No.76757, *Poland*

APPENDIX IX
ROLL OF HONOUR
✝

AIRCREW

Name	Service No	Rank	Age	Origin	Date	Serial
BEFINGER, Mieczysław	PAF P-1896	F/L	29	PAF	16.05.45	KH540
DUNIN, Piotr Jerzy	PAF P-1353	F/O	40	PAF	25.02.42	V9472
HOMAN, Jerzy	PAF P-0757	F/O	39	PAF	25.02.42	V9472
KRUŚ, Leonard	PAF P-2659	F/O	26	PAF	12.02.46	FB210
KUBICA, Franciszek	PAF P-2135	F/L	27	PAF	16.05.45	FB383
PIETRZAK, Aleksander	PAF 783147	W/O	30	PAF	02.08.45	FX876
RAJEWSKI, Eugeniusz Leon	PAF P-1572	F/O	27	PAF	27.12.43	AP240
SADOWSKI, Jerzy Piotr	PAF P-0737	F/O	35	PAF	11.02.42	T6761
SAWICKI, Stanisław	PAF P-1576	F/L	32	PAF	19.03.45	FX860
STRUSIŃSKI, Julian	PAF P-0979	F/O	29	PAF	28.09.44	LF633
ŚWIĘCICKI, Stanisław	PAF 706191	Sgt	26	PAF	15.10.45	KH516

Total: 11

Poland: 11

GROUNDCREW

Name	Service No	Rank	Age	Origin	Date	Serial
PTASZKOWSKI, Antoni	PAF 782728	AC2	27	PAF	14.03.41	-
RADKE, Paweł Marcin	PAF 792736	AC2	27	PAF	14.03.41	-
SOKOŁOWSKI, Zygmunt	PAF 782602	AC2	23	PAF	14.03.41	-

Total: 3

Poland: 3

Even if the Lysander had proved during the Battle of France its vulnerability, Army-Cooperation Command had to soldier on with this type until replacements became available. Thus, No.309 Sqn upon formation received Lysanders as equipment, hoping not to use them again on operations. At first, as markings the aircraft received the Polish Square which was painted behind the RAF roundel (Upper left). Once the Squadron codes were allocated the Polish square remained in the same place obliging the mechanics to paint the individual letter at the same place as the serial. So to avoid the latter being unreadable, the individual letter was painted under the serial. Note on AR-N above the individual letter painted also under the right wing, probably in black. It was common practice in the squadron.
(*Top and left: P. Skulski, bottom: Author's collection*)

Above:
Three Lysanders IIIA during a low-level exercise on a range in Scotland in 1941. The Lysanders are AR-A on the left, AR-N flying on the right, and AR-E, flying at the rear. (*Author's collection*)

Left :
The Lysander could count for its defence on two light machine guns, which had proved in May-June 1940 totally insufficient to offer a real threat against the determination of the German fighter pilots. However these gun remained a good asset to maintain good morale!
(*Chris Szypulewski via*
www.polishsquadronsrembered.com)

After the Lysander, came the Allison-powered Mustang, and this model became the true operational workhorse of Army-Cooperation Command after the interim Tomahawk. Unlike most of the other units of this command, the 309 did not fly with the latter and transitioned direct to the Mustang. Above, AG648 was one of the first Mustangs to be issued to the squadron, and one of the few to have been coded with the letters 'AR', its individual letter was 'E'. Note the black spinner. Later, markings for the Command were altered and squadron codes deleted, but the Polish Square was kept at the same place as can be seen on this unidentified Mustang. The spinner is now painted in white. (*Author's collection*)

As with many Mustang units of Army-Cooperation Command, the operational activity remained low in 1942 -1943, and No.309 Sqn did not perform many sorties with the Mustang. Top and middle, AM214/C, in typical conditions, flying low, with standard markings (spinner and individual letter) of that time.
The squadron was the only RAF unit to have flown on operations with both the Allison Mustang and Merlin-powered Mustang versions. This was due by the change of role of No.309 Sqn, which switched from tactical reconnaissance to a pure fighter unit. However its conversion came too late to allow the squadron to claim many air victories. In the forefront, FZ124/WC-X, a Mustang which was taken on squadron charge after VE-Day and remained in the squadron inventory until disbandment.
(Author's collection)

309 Sqn received two kinds of Mustang IIIs, camouflaged and left in Natural Metal Finish, the two flying together. Above Mustang III FB385/WC-W which was flown by Antoni Murkowski when he claimed a Me262 destroyed and another damaged on 9 April 1945. Below the 309 Sqn pilots are taxiing for another escort mission from Andrews Field during spring 1945. In the forefront it is WC-X, which is probably FB383. As with most Mustang IIIs, none were allocated to a specific pilot, and FB383 was flown by various pilots during spring 1945. Things changed after VE-Day. The air activity remained at a high level in the next few months but decreased as soon as the prospect of disbandment approached. Between VE-Day and January 1947, the squadron Sqn achieved close to 6,000 flying hours on Mustangs.
(P. Skulski - above, www.polishsquadronsrembered.com- below)

Personnel of the Flight "B". Dunino. December 1940.
Identified personel: **1** - Witold Miniszewski, **2** - Maciej Piotrowski, **3** - Waclaw Szypulewski, **4** - Eugeniusz Rajewski († 27.12.43), **5** - Jan Lemieszonek, **6** - Aleksander Lukinski, **7** - Jerzy Golko, **8** - Henryk Wojtkiewicz, **9** - Jozef Kotarba (ground crew chief), **10** - Mieczyslaw Bedzinski (ground crewman?), **11** - Tadeusz Ciula.
(*Chris Szypulewski via www.polishsquadronsrembered.com*)

From L-R - on the engine: Wlodzimierz Klawe, Antoni Murkowski, Teodor Kulecki, Erwin Loska - formerly No.302 Sqn - , Henryk Kaminski, Jan Z Mozołowski, middle row: Mieczysław Befinger (†16.05.45), Franciszek Kubica (†16.05.45) , Stanisław Blok - formerly No.315 Sqn -.Staniskaw
bottom row: Tadeusz Turek, Zygmunt Jaeschke, Stefan Zagroba, Stanislaw Zajchowski, Stanislaw Birtus, *Unkn*, Egon Eisenbach, Jerzy Mencel, Antoni Glowacki, Mieczysław Gorzula - formerly No.302 Sqn - . Andrews Field, Spring 1945.
(*Wojtek Zmyslony - www.polishairforce.pl*)

Group photo of the squadron, from the left - the last row: M. Lewandowski, T. Radkiewicz (Adjudant), L. Krus, E. Block, E. Hanka, K. Zielonka, Z. Jaeschke, S. Zaufal, R. Godlewski, P. Gallus, S. Zagroba, T. Kulecki, E. Eisenbach, E. Loska, B. Czerwinski, T. Wisniewski. Middle row: S. Święcicki, A. Sulikowski, A. Murkowski, R. Kogut, J. Podolski, Front row: Z. Stankiewicz, Cpt. K. Alarm Clock, F / Lt Lewis, J. Polak, Cpt. H. Pietrzak, S. Birtus, British F / O Cutting, Th. Gierycz, J. Mozołowski and T. Turk. Coltishall, the end of September 1945. (*Wojtek Zmyslony - www.polishairforce.pl*)

Below another group of pilotes in 1945, L-R: Stefan Zagroba, Stanislaw Zajkowski, Leonard Krus, Segriusz Czerni. Note the individuak lette 'B' painted under the nose on the white band. (*Wojtek Zmyslony - www.polishairforce.pl*)

When the squadron was converted to a fighter unit, some very experienced pilots progressively joined in as the Flight Commanders and the CO. Left, Wlodzimierz Klawe, a former pre-war PAF pilot who had fought with 113 Esk with which had claimed one confirmed and one probable victory. He later fled to the UK and served with Nos.303 and 316 (Polish) Sqns and added one probable victory. In the middle, Antoni Glowacki, was already a very skilled Polish pilot when the war broke out. He escaped to the UK early in 1940 and fought with No.501 Sqn during the Battle of Britain. He later served with Nos.611 and 308 (Polish) Sqns before being posted as CO of No.309 Sqn in September 1944. He survived the war with nine confirmed victories, one being shared. After the war he continued to serve the RAF and then the RNZAF after he emigrated in New Zealand. Right Karol Birtus, served with many Polish units before joining the squadron. He started his career with No.317 Sqn (September 1942 - March 1944) , then was posted to No.316 Sqn in September 1944 for another tour, arriving at No.309 Sqn in December 1944. He eventually left the squadron at the end of 1946. He later emigrated in Australia. *(via www.polishsquadronsrembered.com)*

Below Jerzy Mencel, the only pilot of the squadron to have been awarded a DFC, on 10.10.45. Mencel had joined the squadron in May 1944. As Birtus, he also seved with No.317 Sqn in 1942 with which he claimed a shared confirmed Fw190 on 15.07.42. He had joined the French Air Force in 1940 but was still under training when France fell and found his way in England and enlisted in the PAF. He became one of the few Polish pilots to shoot down a Me262. He also served with No.308 Sqn during the war. After the war he settled in England. *(Wojtek Zmyslony - www.polishairforce.pl)*

Left: Zygmunt Pistl at left (with two other PAF members) was a rather old pilot in 1940, being born in 1897 and was a pre-war Polish pilot. He fought with the Austro-Hungarian Army during WWI as officer, then fought against the Soviets in 1920-1921. He then became an observer with the Polish Air Force but did not have any active command when the Germans overran Poland. When No.309 Sqn was formed he became the Polish commander of the unit, shadowing W/C Mason before taking command in full of the unit in November 1940 and this until February 1943 despite his age. Until the end of war he was posted to various staff positions and stayed in England after the war. *(via www.polishsquadronsrembered.com)*

Above: Among the few pilots to be posted to the newly-formed No.309 Sqn, Maciej Piotroski was a pre-war Polish bomber pilot who fought the Germans in 1939, and was the CO of 65 Combat Flight. On 17 September he flew to Romania, and then went to France via Hungary, Italy and France before reaching the United Kingdom when France fell. in October 1943 be became the CO of the until April 1944. He later served with No.318 Sqn in 1945. After the war he emigrated to the USA. *(via www.polishsquadronsrembered.com)*

Mieczysław Stanisław Gorzula joined No.309 Sqn in November 1944. He had long service of the RAF as he participated in the Battle of Britain with 607 Sqn. He was a pre-war Polish Air Force member and had joined the RAF early in 1940. After the Battle of Britain he was posted to No.302 (Polish) Sqn, but served also with No.87 Sqn for a short time later on. For his second tour of operations, he joined No.315 (Polish) Sqn in November 1943 as a Flight Commander, then with No.306 (Polish) Sqn before being posted to No.309 Sqn as Flight Commander in November 1944. Although many sorties were flown over years, he claimed his first and only victory in April 1945 while serving with the Squadron. He left the unit in May 1945 and was released from the PAF in January 1947. He later emigrated to Australia. *(via www.polishsquadronsrembered.com)*

Above, Henryk Kaminski who joined the squadron in January 1944. He survived the war and later emigrated to the USA. Below left, Zygmunt Jaeschke who fled from Poland to Hungary at the age of 17 in September 1939. He reached France in 1940 and joined the Polish Army with which he fought during the Battle of France. He was evacuated to the UK with his regiment. He volunteered to serve with the PAF in 1943 and after having served in second line units joined No.309 Sqn in September 1944. After the war he returned in Poland. Below right, Mieczyslaw Lewandowski who enlisted in the PAF in 1930. In 1939 he was flying instructor and was recalled to front-line units and served with 42 Light Bomber Flight. He fled to France but was still under training when France fell. His flight instructor skill make him well suited to serve in RAF flying schools and he joined his operational posting (309 Sqn) only in 1943. In 1945 he served with CFS as CFI Assistant. In 1947 he chose to return in Poland. *(all via www.polishsquadronsrembered.com)*

Antoni Murkowski was born in Germany of Polish parents. When the war broke out he was undertaking training to become a bomber pilot with the Polish Air Force. He escaped to the UK in 1940 and served first as a staff pilot with No.6 AACU between July 1941 and January 1942. He started his fighter pilot career with No.316 (Polish) Sqn in September 1942 and remained with it for the next two years, with which he claimed one confirmed and probable Fw190 and four V-1s. After a short rest, he joined No.309 Sqn in December 1944 and became one of most successful pilots of the unit in claiming two confirmed victories and one Me262 damaged. He remained with the RAF after the war retiring from the service a Squadron Leader in 1975.

The fate of some Poles was far from enviable, like Wladislasw Sliwinski. He had fought with Polish fighters units since October 1942 and served with Nos. 306, 302, 303 Sqns - with which he claimed a Bf109 destroyed - and again No.302 Sqn, but joined the squadron well after VE-Day, in January 1946. He moved back to Poland with his wife - a former Polish WAAF - but was soon arrested with his wife in June 1948 by the Communists, put in jail and tortured. He was eventually convicted on espionage charges and executed on 15.02.51. (all via www.polishsquadronsrembered.com)

SUMMARY OF THE OPERATIONAL ACTIVITY
No.309 (POLISH) SQUADRON

A/C types	First sortie	Last sortie	Total sorties	Tot Sub-type	Lost Ops	Lost Acc	A/C lost	Claims	V-1	Pilot †	PoWs	Eva.
LYSANDER III	-	-	-	-	-	4	4	-	-	2	-	-
MUSTANG I	05.12.42	03.11.44	388	388	1	6	7	-	-	1	-	-
HURRICANE II	25.04.44	09.10.44	204	204	-	1	1	-	-	1	-	-
MUSTANG III	23.12.44	25.04.45	687	687	1	10	11	4.0	-	6	-	-
Others												
TIGER MOTH	-	-	-	-	-	1	1	-	-	1	-	-
OTHER CAUSES	-	-	-	-	-	-	-	-	-	-	-	-
COMPILATION	05.12.42	25.04.45	1,279	1,279	2	22	24	4.0	-	11	-	-

MAIN AWARDS

DSO: -

DFC: 1

DFM: -

Points of interest :
- The only Army Co-Operation Command Polish squadron.
- The only Mustang unit to have flown the two main models, Allison and Merlin powered.

Unsolved mystery:
None

Statistics:
- Lost one aircraft every 640 sorties [Mustang I: 388, Hurricane II: -, Mustang III: 687]

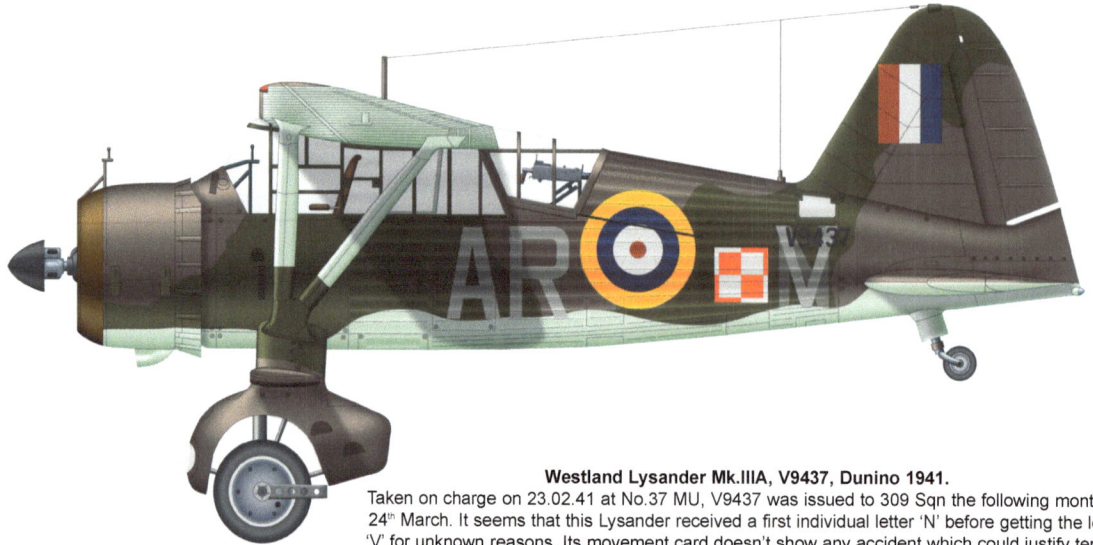

Westland Lysander Mk.IIIA, V9437, Dunino 1941.
Taken on charge on 23.02.41 at No.37 MU, V9437 was issued to 309 Sqn the following month on 24th March. It seems that this Lysander received a first individual letter 'N' before getting the letter 'V' for unknown reasons. Its movement card doesn't show any accident which could justify temporary repairs out of squadron facilities. However V9437 did have a Cat.B accident in September 1942 and was sent for repairs and never to come back as the Squadron was giving up Lysanders by that date. It was eventually struck off charge on 23.10.43.

Westland Lysander Mk.IIIA, V9544, Dunino 1941.
Like V9437, V9544 was new when it was issued to 309 Sqn in spring 1941. Same camouflage - Dark Earth/Dark Green, Sky undersurfaces - with the one oddity of 309 Sqn, the presence of the individual letter under the starboard wing - 'O'. Photographic evidence shows that in 1941, all the Lysanders had their individual letters repeated under the right wing.

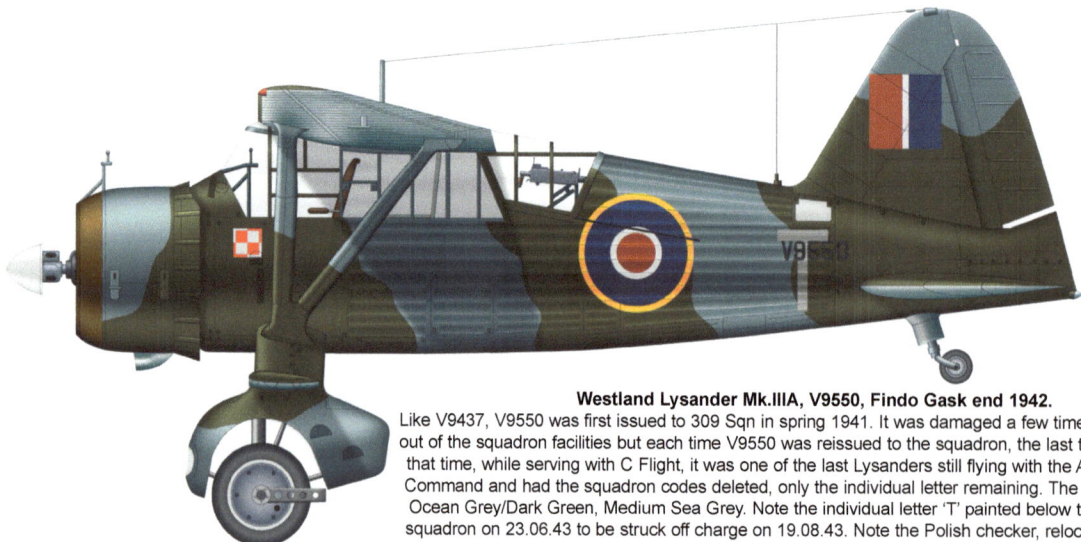

Westland Lysander Mk.IIIA, V9550, Findo Gask end 1942.
Like V9437, V9550 was first issued to 309 Sqn in spring 1941. It was damaged a few times and was repaired out of the squadron facilities but each time V9550 was reissued to the squadron, the last time on 31.12.42. At that time, while serving with C Flight, it was one of the last Lysanders still flying with the Army Co-Operation Command and had the squadron codes deleted, only the individual letter remaining. The camouflage is now Ocean Grey/Dark Green, Medium Sea Grey. Note the individual letter 'T' painted below the serial. It left the squadron on 23.06.43 to be struck off charge on 19.08.43. Note the Polish checker, relocated in the forward part of the aircraft and the white spinner.

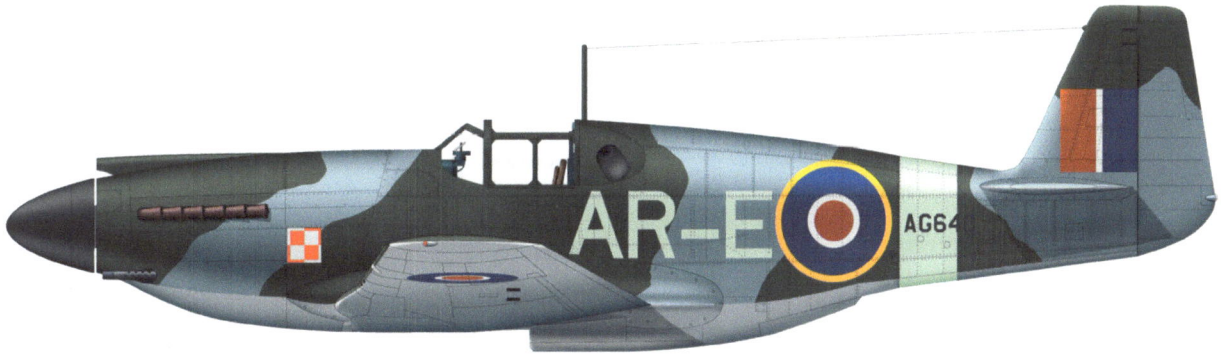

North American Mustang Mk.I AG648, Dunino, August 1942.
Arriving in the UK in May 1942, AG648 was modified and a camera installed behind the cockpit before being issued to 309 Sqn on 19.08.42. It was one of the first Mustang Mk.Is to be issued to this unit. In summer 1942, squadron codes were still worn inside the Army Co-Operation Command, but as the fuselage of the Mustang was not well fitted to have codes, roundel and individual letter painted in the regular manner, the roundel had to be relocated to the rear and codes relocated forwards with a dash separating the squadron codes and individual letter. It was also a common practice within the other Mustang units at that time. By the end of the year, the squadron codes had disappeared and this problem was solved. It remained with the squadron until March 1944 after having completed 16 sorties.

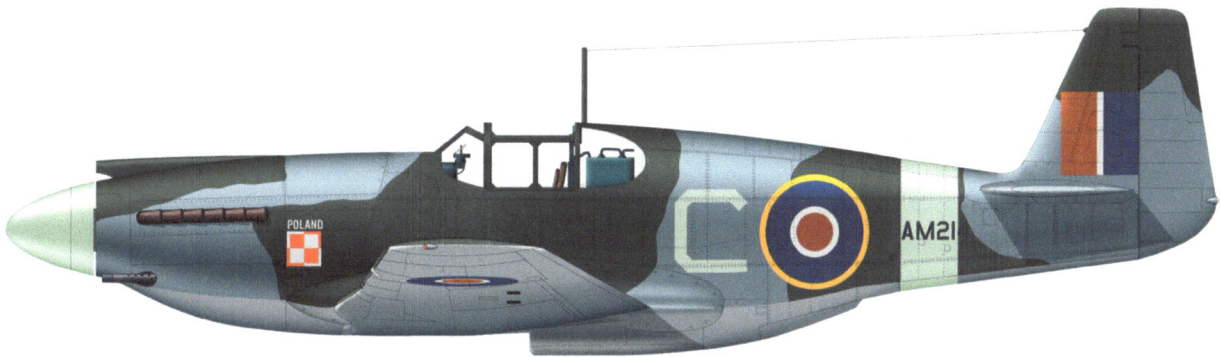

North American Mustang Mk.I AM2140, Snailwell (UK), Autumn 1943.
Arriving in the UK in July 1942, it served at Speke (believed to be as a liaison aircraft) before being issued to 309 Sqn on 09.08.43. Coded 'C' it completed 15 sorties between 16.08.43 and 04.01.44. Sent to storage on 17.03.44 at No.33 MU, it later served with 168 and 26 Sqns and survived the war to be struck off charge
in June 1945.

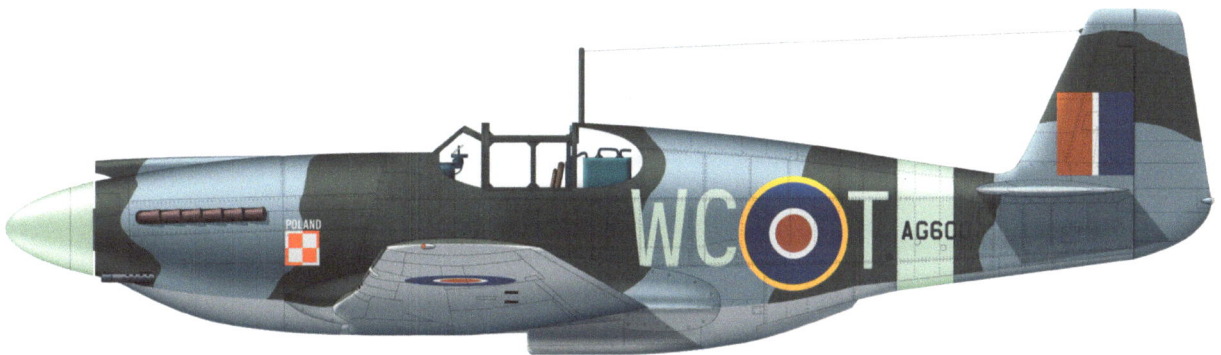

North American Mustang Mk.I AG600, Peterhead (UK), October 1944.
To facilitate the conversion to the Mustang III, 309 Sqn received some Mustang Is in September 1944 while the ageing Hurricane Mk.IICs were leaving the squadron, allowing the Mustang I to return to the interception role, one of the few occasion it did so. AG600 arrived in the UK on 20.02.42 and served with 225, 268, 231 Sqns and later with No.41 OTU when it was issued to 309 Sqn on 08.09.44. Its service with the squadron was short and left the unit for 26 Sqn on 09.11.44. It survived the war to be struck off charge in June 1945.

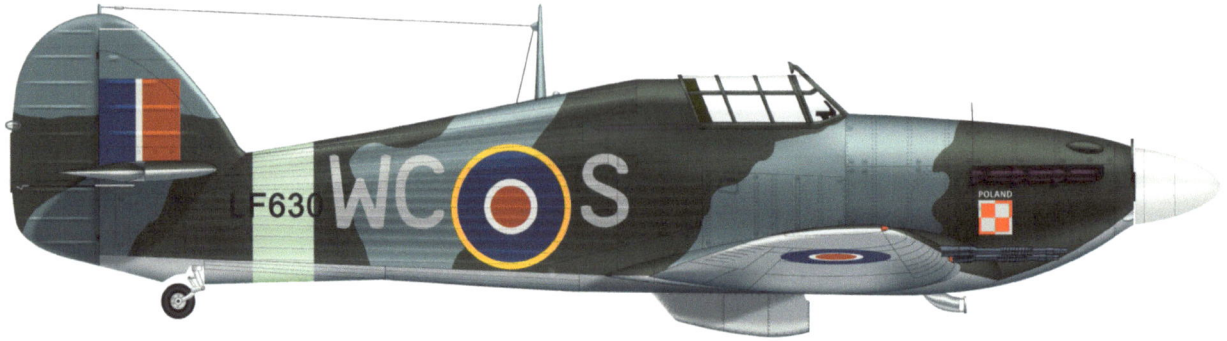

Hawker Hurricane Mk.IIC LF630, Drem (UK), Spring 1944.
When 309 Sqn switched to the interceptor role, it exchanged its Mustang Mk.Is for obsolete Hurricane Mk.IICs to help to familiarise the pilots with fighter tactics. LF630 was one of the last Hurricanes built and had been taken on RAF charge on 01.03.44 and issued to the squadron one month later. It left the squadron on 13.10.44 and later served with Com. Flight in the BAFO from June 1945 onwards. It was struck off charge in July 1947.

North American Mustang Mk.III FZ111, F/L Myeczyslaw Gorzula, Andrews Fields (UK), Spring 1945.
Built as P-51B-5-NA 43-6411, it was shipped to the UK on S.S. *Menacy* arriving on 24.10.43. It first served with 65 Sqn from January 1944 until end of March '44 when it was sent for repairs. Repaired it was held at No.20 MU until being issued to 309 Sqn on 28.10.44. It became the mount of F/L Gorzula in February 1945. It seems that FZ111 was kept as spare aircraft and used at first for training and other minor tasks but F/L Gorzula claimed a Me262 on 09.04.45 with this aircraft. It served with the squadron until January 1946.

North American Mustang Mk.III SR420, F/L Jan Mozołowski, Andrews Fields (UK), December 1944.
Built as P-51B-1-NA 42-12480, it was transferred to the RAF in UK on 29.03.44 as part of a batch of 34 P-51Bs from 8th AF stock. It was modified to RAF standard (which include the Mustang identification bands) and put into storage at No.20 MU in June 1944, and as with all the B-1 model it didn't have the extra dorsal fin near the tail. It was issued to 309 Sqn on 28.10.44 and was one of the first Mustang IIIs taken on charge by the squadron. SR420 became the regular mount of F/L Mozołowski who flew it during the first Mustang III mission of the squadron (RAMROD 1414) on 23.12.44. It remained on squadron charge until 26.04.45 and never flew again with an operational squadron before eventually struck off charge on 24.02.47.

North American Mustang Mk.III KH516, F/L Jerzy Menzel, Andrews Fields (UK), Spring 1945.

Built as P-51C-10-NT 44-10918, it was shipped on S.S. *Nicholson* and arrived in the on 17.08.44. After some more modifications, KH516 was stored at No.38 MU from 30.11.44 onwards and was issued to 316 (Polish) Sqn on 27.02.45, soon cancelled to go to 309 Sqn instead two days later. But it seems that it arrived some weeks later as its first flight is recorded on 03.04.45. It was replacing a previous WC-F, FX885. In the last stage of the war, KH516 became the regular mount of F/L Mencel who claimed a Me262 on 09.04.45 while flying this aircraft. It is not known however what the port side looks like, with a possible swastika "kill" marking. KH516 served with the squadron until being destroyed in a crash on 15.10.45, killing its pilot (see aircraft lost in accident).

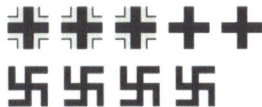

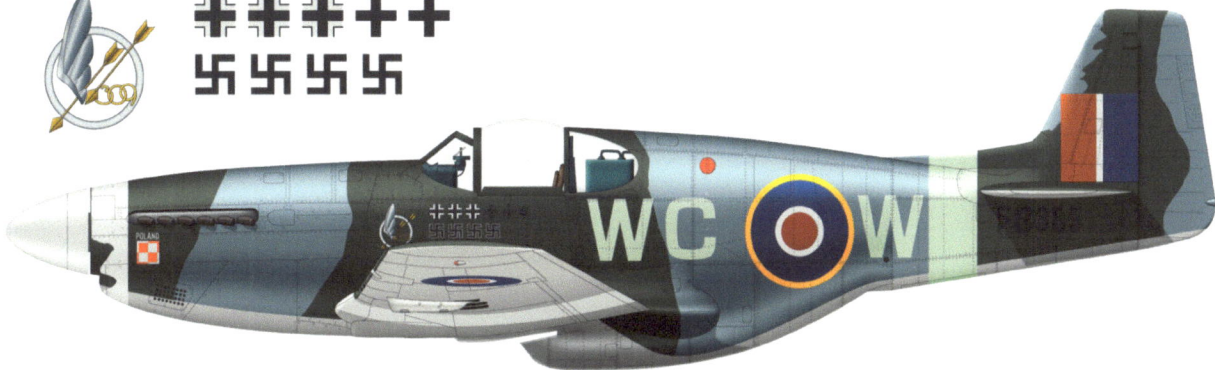

North American Mustang Mk.III FB385, W/O Antoni Murkowski, Andrews Fields (UK), Summer 1945.

Built as P-51C-1-NT 42-103265, it was shipped on S.S. *British Flony* and arrived in the UK on 04.05.44. After some more modifications, FB385 was stored at No.20 MU a couple of days only before being issued to 316 (Polish) Sqn on 25.06.44. It served with this squadron for a while and it seems to have also served with 65 Sqn between unrecorded dates before arriving with 309 Sqn in March 1945 to replace a former WC-W, FX853. The intensive use of this Mustang can be noticed by the faded paint in places. It became the regular mount of Antoni Murkowski and he claimed a Me262 with this aircraft on 09.04.45. FB385 is seen here during summer 1945 when the pilots took the time to add some personal artwork. FB385 served served with the squadron until its disbandment. As most if not all camouflaged Mustangs IIIs of the squadron, the indivudual letter is believed to be repeated under the nose on the white nose band.

North American Mustang Mk.III FX876, Andrews Fields (UK), Summer 1945.

Built as P-51B-1-NA 42-12146, it was shipped to the UK on S.S. *F.J. Wolfe* arriving on 23.09.43. Its first operational assignment came on 18.04.44 when it was sent to 316 (Polish) Sqn where it remained until mid-summer. In August 1944, it was flying with FIU and in November was serving 129 Sqn until issued to 309 Sqn on 24.05.45. It is not known at what stage FX876 was stripped of its camouflage and identification bands, but most probably while serving with the squadron. This aircraft was destroyed on the following 2ⁿᵈ August in a flying accident, its pilot escaping injuries (see aircraft lost in accident). Note that that at some stage an extra dorsal fin has been added, a fin the early B models didn't had. If it seems that most if not all camouflaged Mustang IIIs have their individual letter repeated under the nose, nothing is sure for the NMF Mustang IIIs of the Squadron.

29

1922-

The Supermarine
SPITFIRE Mk.V
in the Far East

Vol
Type Desig

Phil H. LISTEMANN

Fighter Leaders
of the RAF, RAAF, RCAF, RNZAF & SAAF in WW2

Volume I

Phil H. Listemann

AT WAR.
STUDY, HISTORY AND STATISTICS

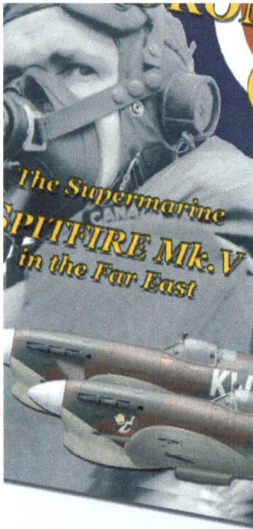

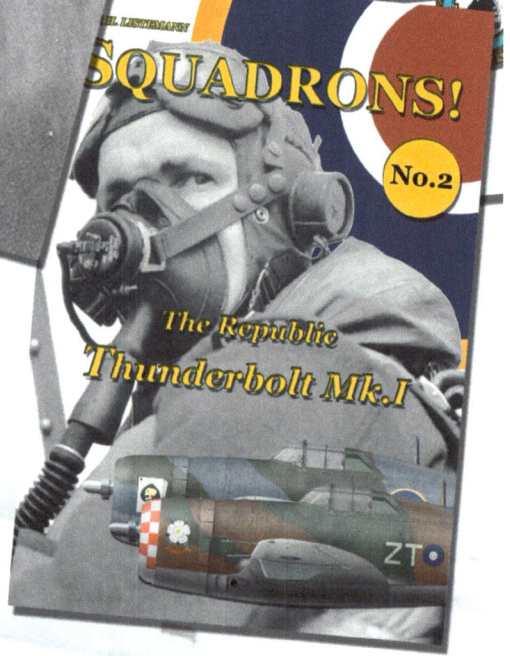

No.137 Squadron
1941 - 1945

SQUADRONS!

No.2

The Republic
Thunderbolt Mk.I

www.RAF-IN-COMBAT.com

- USN Aircraft 1922-1962 -
- Squadrons! -
- RAF, Dominion and Allied squadrons at War -
- Allied Wings -
RAF, DOMINION & ALLIED SQUADRONS
AT WAR: - **Famous squadrons of WW2** -
STUDY, HISTORY AND STATISTICS
- Fighter Leaders -

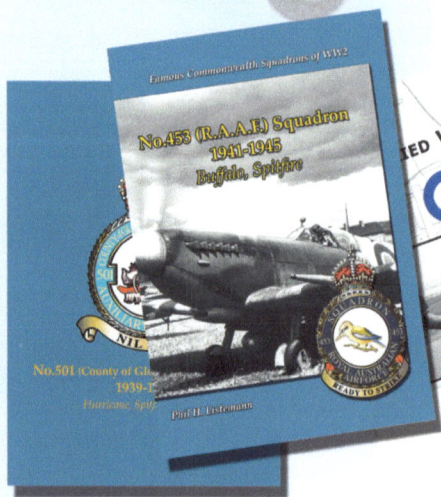

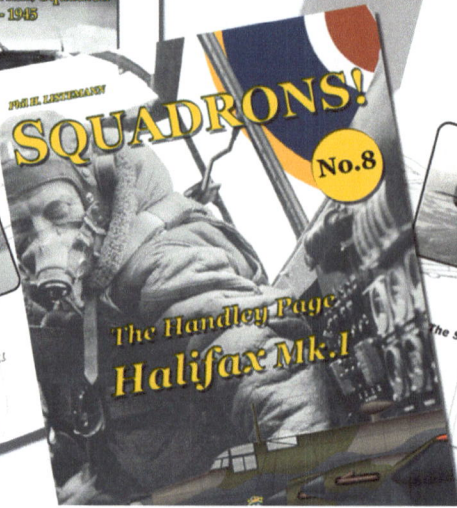

Famous Commonwealth Squadrons of WW2

No.453 (R.A.A.F.) Squadron
1941-1945
Buffalo, Spitfire

No.131 (County of Kent) Squadron
1941 - 1945

LIED WINGS

IED WINGS

SQUADRONS!

No.8

The Handley Page
Halifax Mk.I

ALLIED WINGS

No.501 (County of Gl
1939-
Hurricane, Spit
Phil H. Listemann

Short SINGAPORE III

Phil M. Listemann

No.18
The Supermarine SPITFIRE
F.24
Phil H. LISTEMANN

www.ingramcontent.com/pod-product-compliance
Lightning Source LLC
LaVergne TN
LVHW072122070426
835511LV00002B/65